Fix It, Twins!

Max and Min are twins.

Look at us!
We are twins.

Max

Min

Min has a skill.

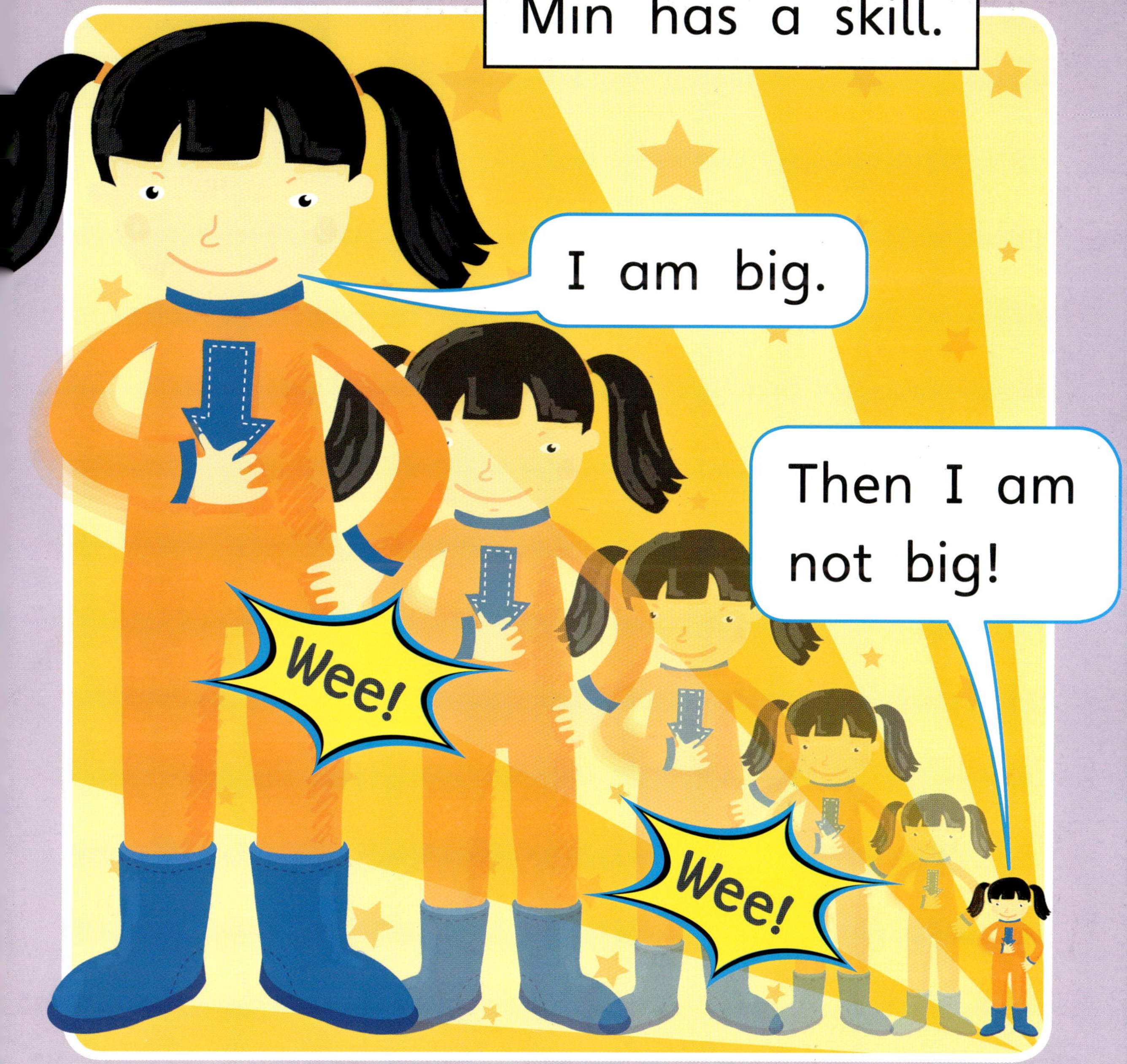

Max has a skill too.

This is my skill.
I can get big.

Zoom!

Zoom!

The clock is high up, but Max can fix it.

Tug!

Look at his foot!
Min can help.

Keep still!

Max has a light bulb.
He can fix the light.

The boats
might crash!

The queen has a bad pain in a tooth.

Min is not big.
She can fix the tooth.

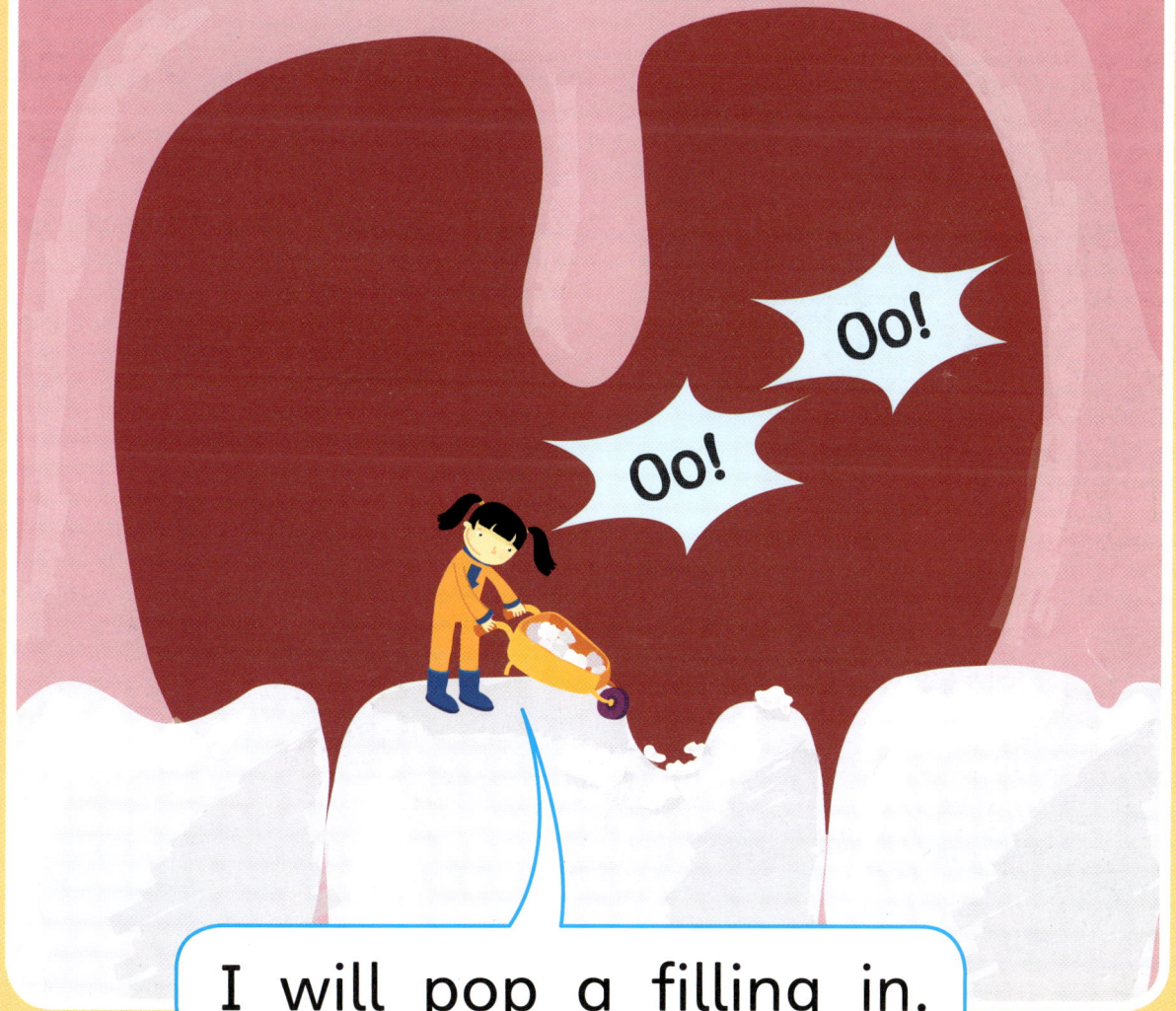

Oo!

Oo!

I will pop a filling in.

Twins are the best!